The
Little
Book
of **Big**
Advice

Enlightening
Ideas for
Bellydance
Professionals

by Tava Naiyin

PHOTOGRAPHY: Adrian Buckmaster
COVER and BOOK DESIGN: © 2015 Susan Gravdahl Parsons

To my husband, gig roadie, music editor, driver, occasional chef, partner and best friend, Pete. Sharing this strange and exciting life with you is a true gift. Please forgive 15 years of glitter in the strangest of places.

And to my mother, my original dance partner, for planting these seeds of creativity. I would surely be lost without you in my corner.

Special Offer!
The Art of Negotiating Rates for Professional Bellydancers: FREE

Thank you for purchasing *Little Book of Big Advice: Enlightening Ideas for Budding Bellydance Professionals*. If you're interested in this topic, we invite you to sign up for our newsletter at BellydancebyTava.com and receive a link to Tava's recording: "The Art of Negotiating Rates for Professional Bellydancers" for FREE! This bonus recording is an excerpt from Tava's Mentorship Program, an interactive training (limited to 8 dancers at a time) that covers more in-depth information for aspiring bellydancers. Participants will receive customized feedback, video links, an hour one-on-one Q & A chat with Tava, gig checklists, & more. Serious dancers are encouraged to apply. Just visit the above link and click on Mentorship Program.

TABLE OF CONTENTS

f you're reading this book, chances are you can recall that moment when you first fell in love with this dance. Perhaps you saw a performance as a child and it planted a seed. Maybe you were already an adult when you stumbled into your first bellydance class and felt immediately hooked by the movements. Whatever the case, no one can deny that there is something magical about this art form. Aside from its obvious beauty, there is a mystery to it that continues to unfold the longer we do it. A bellydancer will take everyone in the room on a journey that is exciting, mysterious, emotional and playful. What's not to love about that?

If we all agree that this is an easy dance to fall in love with, perhaps we can also agree that not everyone has the right skills and temperament to make a successful career of it. My intention is not to be controversial or squash anyone's dreams but to paint a clear picture of what is involved in "going pro" so people can make informed choices. My goal is also to help prevent a decline in industry standards and to promote professionalism. Not everybody has a lengthy list of mentors to run things by and may unknowingly make a choice, offer a quote or perform in a way that promotes a stereotype, undercuts other professionals or offends a culture.

To offer a broader perspective, I have asked some of my students, friends, colleagues and a few of my mentors to share their insights. I am truly grateful to Andrea (New York), Angelica (Québec), Maria (California), Miki (Kansas), Riskallah (Connecticut), Sira (New York), and Zaina (Globetrotter), for lending their voices to this book. My hope is that aspiring bellydancers will read this, refer to it, question it, or even blatantly disagree. In any case, any worthy book provokes thought and I am so invested in this content that I offer my respect to anyone who thinks about these topics and forms a well thought out opinion, regardless of whether it differs from mine.

I wrote this book for anyone who loves Oriental dance, modern Egyptian style, Turkish Oryantal, Raqs Sharqi, Folkloric Arabic dances, American Cabaret, Lebanese style, Gulf dances and any other genre, category or description that relates. I've geared content particularly to the aspiring professionals who are at the semi-pro level and contemplating their options.

These are the dancers who may have done a handful of 25-minute performance sets that successfully entertained an audience. But, perhaps, their next audience includes Persian and Tunisian couples who want their dancer to "incorporate a bit from each of their cultures" into a show. (This is an actual request I received). The audience after that might specifically request candle tray because they saw it on YouTube, and the next may be "firmly against all those silly balance props" (another actual quote from a client). We have to embrace these challenges and appreciate that they help us grow as artists. This is an art that rewards us with feelings of progress and technical mastery—only until we face the next challenge. That is a large part of its appeal.

I hope to reach those dancers who have a few years under their hip scarves in what I would describe as a time of confidence building. This is when a dancer starts to carve out a name for her or himself in a community with haflas, opening slots and maybe some restaurant shows. This may also be a time when people stop taking weekly classes and run the risk of feeling over-confident. By and large, however, it's also when the role of the mentor changes and these dancers are given more specific direction and homework to foster their learning.

The semi-pro must remain grounded, hungry for opportunities, curious about the cultures and broaden her or his scope to include such things as non-obvious folkloric styles, appropriate costuming, and also shaping their own style as a dancer. There is no specific amount of time to remain in this stage and some people stay here for their entire dancing career. I think this is the best phase of all because it's where the richest learning occurs, without the pressures of trying to run a business.

When I was a semi-pro, I performed at the wedding of a friend with two other dancers. I got great feedback from the guests (aka "lay people") who were full of compliments for me. This is the stage where I learned that people like to compliment performers. Nobody is going to come up to you and say, "Your performance was so-so." Please, stay humble and take compliments graciously. Beauty, sparkles, props and smiles go a long way, but we can't stop there.

Transform me into the character I wanted to be.

Photography: Bill Winters

I. In the beginning

hen I was in pre-school, a guest dancer came to teach a bellydance class for the girls who were interested. She brought in these fantastic coined hip scarves and I felt my little 4-year-old self shake with excitement and curiosity. Well, she didn't have enough scarves for everyone and so I did the movements with great disappointment, fighting back the tears, because I didn't have the appropriate "costume" to transform me into the character I wanted to be. My only performance credit to date was as a dancing Christmas present, (where I stood in a large box with holes cut out for my legs, arms and head). Those coined hip scarves were far more captivating than my cardboard. So, in a nutshell, that was my entire experience with bellydance in the 1970s.

For several years after that I studied jazz, ballet and gymnastics. My parents drove me to lessons, sat through numerous recitals and grew accustomed to my whirling around our home and doing splits in doorways. Somewhere around age 16, adolescent pressures took hold and I decided I didn't want to dance anymore. I stopped ballet at the first sign of curves and decided I was "too cool" for dance class. Ironically, I believe it is a time when young women need dance the most, but I didn't know that at the time. This experience has shaped my passion for teaching teens. There is something profoundly satisfying about sharing a dance of body awareness, community and celebration with that age group.

Fast forward to the late 1990s when I worked with a variety show that featured the best of underground NYC entertainment. There were comedians, magicians, neo-burlesque dancers, a contortionist, a sword swallower and many other acts that blended the bizarre with the beautiful. A regular performer in this show was Andrea, a bellydancer. The audience, which was an odd collection of people from all walks of life, was immediately transfixed by Andrea's hypnotic entrance. Concealed by her veil, her performance unfolded like a story. While watching her shows, I realized that this dance wasn't only excited shaking, but a tool for transforming the energy in the room. It was elegant, ethereal, emotional and contained subtleties that left the audience wanting more. I had no idea how rich this dance could be, having seen only shimmying smiles in movie clips. As a shy introvert, but one who has always loved a stage, I knew I wanted to dive head first into to something that powerful and beautiful.

Like many, I was afraid to start classes because I was embarrassed about my lack of ability. Insecurities were born and I didn't want to look foolish in front of a group of people who, I assumed, would all be good at a dance I didn't know how to do. I had danced my entire life and worked hard to earn a front-row spot in performances, but that only made it harder for me to contemplate being a beginner. Finally, after watching every DVD I could find and asking friends who took Andrea's class to show me what they had learned, I developed the courage to start classes.

In class, I had to unlearn a lot and break a few bad postural habits I'd developed without knowing it. I also had to expose my vulnerability and conquer my shyness on a whole new level. Other dance forms require a lifted chin with a smile but that's really easy to hide behind. This one required an authentic expression that was driven by the rich music that supported it. Yikes! Not easy.

About eight months into my beginner class, I attended a retreat for dancers and drummers. Because I felt like a reasonably coordinated beginner, I figured I was ready for the next step. That was where I met the intermediate class and became completely intimidated by what they were doing and how much they knew, particularly with regard to how they danced to live drumming. When Andrea had given me the green light to move up, I happily did so, however, there were some movements and concepts that I didn't have enough experience with. I worked with Andrea privately to fill in the gaps. I began attending workshops at this level to supplement my training. Standing in the back, WAY in the back, I absorbed as much as I could. I assumed this would be a hobby for a long time and never had any ambitions to become a performer, instructor or choreographer. I'm grateful for this slow start because it helped me form the deepest respect for the dance.

At some point, Andrea asked if I would like the opening slot at Le Figaro, the former cafe in the West Village.

Le Fig, as we had called it, was a very special place on Sunday nights. Here, Scott Wilson and a rotating lineup of musicians would perform and invite 3 to 4 bellydancers to join them. Typically, they asked a teacher or two to headline the night and a couple of their students would open the show with a mini set. Living in Manhattan and spending almost every Sunday at Figaro was such important training. The level of skill I witnessed on these dance-filled nights humbled me. When it was my turn to perform, I actually thought my legs might fail me. Thankfully, they didn't. I came alive. I learned how to communicate with the band dancing in those opening slots, how to pace myself and how to engage a crowd. Most importantly, I saw the difference in energy when the headlining dancer came on. I could clearly see where I needed to improve. When I finally headlined my own show, and supported my students through their nerves, it was the first time I really felt like a professional.

Over the years I've collected additional teachers and there are some I always clear my calendar for when they come to town. I am lucky to have learned from so many people I admire, but I always go back to the beginning and reflect on how fortunate I was to have chosen the right teacher to help me build a solid foundation. The beginning paves the way for everything that follows.

II. Now

At present, I'm a teacher, performer and choreographer. I wake up and look at my calendar to see where I am sup- posed to be on a given night and calculate travel times between engagements. It is unpredictable, fulfilling and exciting. I have students who are brand-new beginners, as well as some who have professional costumes and are slowly making the transition to semi-professional status. More recently, I have a handful of Skype students in other parts of the country (and one sweet gal in Germany), and I have taught a variety of workshops outside of my state.

I have performed for fantasy-based theatrical shows, store openings, cultural festivals, museums, weddings, divorce parties, christenings, fancy corporate galas and backyard parties. I look back on my experiences and, whether dancing on stage to a spoken word artist or in a music video, each called for a different skill set and brought out a different quality to my dancing. This is the fun part of my job and I believe the key to a long-term relationship with dance is to embrace the variety.

Most recently, I have taken on the role of mentor. It's a strange feeling to be on the other side of this relationship. I'm no longer the baby in the business and have amassed enough experiences to be able to share them with newer professionals. At least several times per week, I receive a call or email from someone I know or don't know, with questions. Most of the time, they come in response to something I've written on my blog (dancingtava.word-press.com). Other times, they are local dancers who know me. This is part of why I felt compelled to put as much information as I can in one place. I'm certainly not fin-ished studying, but I'm happy to share what I've learned along the way.

At the moment, my typical week involves teaching six classes and two private lessons, practice for myself at least a few days a week, attending rehearsals for Elena Lentini's Caravanseria Dance Theater, and have anywhere from one to six performances. There were times when I did more and there have been times when I did less. I confess to having a minor addiction to my phone because I know that an inquiry often leads to a job and if I don't respond in a timely manner, I could miss an opportunity. Clients call with an inquiry and if I don't make that pitch right then and there, it is a few hundred dollars of unearned income. This is just a reality of the job.

I left a very stable job as a career counselor and disability services coordinator in order to allow as much time as possible for dance. I'm fortunate enough to have a supportive husband and family. My non-dance friends sometimes express frustration at my lack of availability. Some relationships have suffered, but this is a real consequence of the dancer's schedule. We teach in the evenings and perform on weekends when most people enjoy free time. Finding a balance between work and life is challenging and the sacrifices are not always easy. If at all possible, it really helps to make it a family affair. For instance, my husband often attends my shows and edits my music; my father works the door for any shows that I produce; and my mother attends my classes. It takes a village.

When I have free time, I am often watching YouTube looking at some of my inspirations, or choreographing in my head. I also attend as many performances as I can to support my friends or colleagues and the venues that showcase our art. In reality, this is all part of the job. Many vacations are spent visiting dance friends in other parts of the country and teaching or taking classes. You can imagine that a relationship in which the partner isn't 100% on board would make this a rather impossible arrangement. I am lucky that my husband has formed friendships with the spouses and partners of other dancers who we visit, and that he takes pride in helping me advance my career. And of course, we aim for at least one date night per week to keep a bit of sanity in our lives. If the goal is artistic fulfillment, lifelong learning, building community, performing and teaching, this is what it takes and there are plenty of people who do more than I do in this regard.

As to the physical challenges of my job, I spend a good deal of time on self-care. This means dedicated time on my foam roller, receiving regular reflexology, proper nutrition for energy, massage, stretching and strengthening to avoid injury. I have had temporary bouts of pain and inflammation from overuse, but, thankfully, nothing chronic. Many of my dance friends who reach this level of experience have long-term problems with their knees, back, feet or neck. There is no guarantee that I will be able to avoid these problems, but I try my best to be smart about knowing my limits. This is something you may not consider at all when starting a career as a professional bellydancer, but the awareness starts to creep in that your ability to shimmy, do level changes, swing a cane or toss your hair around is rooted in being free of pain.

Lastly, I need time to nurture myself emotionally. I'm a sensitive person, so a disrespectful audience or insensitive comment can affect me more than it should. I've been called trash, asked to give lap dances, and had audiences try and stuff dollar bills in inappropriate places. I am quick with witty comebacks and never show my hurt, but I'd be lying if I said that I never left a gig in tears. This is extremely rare, of course, and it's just a consequence of caring so much that it leaves me vulnerable. I would never show this emotion to a client, but sometimes it just takes its toll. I cope by chatting with someone I love to help me process it and then let it go. That being said, people have said the kindest things to me during and after shows. This past New Year's Eve, after my fifth performance of the night, I had a stranger approach me in the bathroom and pay me one of the best compliments of my entire dance life. There are so many beautiful moments. Way too many to even remember. A lot of people hug me, so I think I'm exactly where I need to be.

III. Looking ahead

I'm aware that I cannot maintain this schedule long-term. This job puts a premium on youth and at a certain point, the phone will stop ringing for gigs. It's important to prepare for that transition. I know people who actively gig at 50+, and they look fantastic. I have also seen people who have not thought beyond their bellydance careers and are trying hard to cling to it when the opportunities are fewer and fewer. It is hard to imagine competing for the same jobs with dancers who are 30 years younger. That being said, most of my favorite dancers to watch are well over 40. There is nothing more artistically satisfying than watching someone who has decades of dedication to an art form, release it on a stage. I should be so lucky to reach that level. I believe that when confidence is paired with experience, it is a really beautiful time in a dancer's life.

I was recently chatting with one of my teachers, who is in her 70s. She said, "Tava, you won't ever stop dancing, so don't worry." I imagine my contributions will be different and I won't be gigging for money, but sharing art for the sake of sharing. Maybe this is why older performers are among my favorite to watch. They are no longer in the art vs. commerce struggle. Maybe this is our gift at the end of our careers. These dancers have earned the right to dance to however they choose.

So, how can I set myself on that track? By cultivating other opportunities for work. Rather than wait until there is a decline in my popularity for gigs, I am spending time on my other streams of income. I do not want to fall into the trap of being unprepared. I have slowly returned to the career counseling field (part-time) and I'm hoping to maintain space in my life for both passions as long as possible. This is my goal and I'm fortunate enough to have some role models—people who have managed to achieve this—so I know it can be done if I'm smart about it.

I loved Sundays at my Arabic grandparents' house.

Photographer: Kvon

Riskallah Riyad (owner, Connecticut Dance Oasis) is a brilliant example of how someone with over 40 years in bellydance remains deeply committed to loving and learning her art.

Riskallah, Connecticut

"I loved Sundays at my Arabic grandparents' house, where we congregated to dance and listen to music. I loved the applause my little sister received as she migrated from one family member to the next, doing her interpretation of a shimmy.

There in my childhood began a lifelong love of the music, the dance and the culture. Pursuing this passion years later, I studied in NYC (there were no teachers in Connecticut at the time) with the great Ibrahim Farrah.

Already a teacher by profession, the segue to teaching dance and performing was a natural step. For more than 40 years, I have pursued this dance with the passion of a lover, becoming its happy prisoner as I challenge myself to be better. We owe it to our audiences, our students, and ourselves to be the best that we can be, and to elevate the art. In my case, I also want to honor my heritage. I continue to study, take private lessons, sponsor master workshops, develop new ideas and attend theater, one of my sources of dance inspiration."

I. Don't rush it

Maybe it's just human nature to want to master and move on. We like to conquer a challenge and then feel proud of ourselves. There is also the allure of performing that makes people want to rush on through the learning and dive into the first hookah lounge that will have us. Allow me a moment to climb on to my soapbox and shout, "Don't call yourself a professional bellydancer before you are ready!" We work so hard to elevate the perception of our dance and to educate the public to dispel the lingering stereotypes and be taken seriously as an art form. We may never have the prestige of a ballet dancer, but isn't it better to say that our performers have trained appropriately before working in public?

After performing in student showcases and haflas, I had to take my lumps and learn that I needed better eye contact, needed to lift my chin more when dancing to an entrance, and I definitely made a few costume mistakes. I received feedback from my teacher and sometimes felt really proud of myself, only to watch the video of my performance and feel that I was not improving. The last things to develop are expressive arms and hands while the hips are working. When it comes to arms, most of us look sort of like lazy scarecrows for the first year. It doesn't matter that we are offered work before we are worthy of working.

The purpose of this section is to highlight the best reasons why to delay the gratification, and to perform only when you're truly competent instead of when a budget-conscious venue wants you. I went through my own odd introduction to the world of bellydance performance so I empathize with those who are feeling the temptation to share your budding skills with a happy crowd.

Our dance suffers from more stereotypes than you can imagine. For this reason, when pseudo-bellydancers perform it, they are likely sending the wrong messages to the public. Oftentimes these messages are hyper-sexualized, overly flashy, or so full of fusion it's hard to know what it is. The audience tells a friend, "Yeah I saw a bellydancer who was also a contortionist who was breathing fire and dancing to hip hop on roller blades." This sounds very entertaining, but put in the same category as what I do, it's a completely different art. If the public learns to expect bellydance with a fire-breathing roller blader, there goes years of serious training in favor of tricks that have nothing to do with our dance.

Here is my confession. Because I had a dance background with some variety, I began performing fairly early on in my bellydance life. I thought, because the show included a poet backed by a live blues band (and one could assume that authenticity was not their top priority), that it would operate like the rest of my dance life. I did my best to represent the dance in the best way I could, with appropriate costuming, and it helped shape my stage presence, audience interaction, and work with live musicians. But there's no denying it was on-the-job training. I didn't do truly authentic bellydance gigs for several years.

If you are young, pretty, and have a half-way decent bellydance vocabulary, chances are opportunities may come your way sooner than you are actually ready. It seems so exciting to put on the glamour and perform for a group of strangers. In reality, it is exciting. But getting there too soon is like trying to have a conversation in a foreign language that you're only just learning. Maybe we have enough words to string together a sentence, but there's a very good chance we will say the wrong thing without realizing it. It's better to practice with people who can give us the right feedback for as long as we need to.

If this sounds like I'm trying to squash creativity and fusion dance styles, I promise this is not my goal. I love that I live so close to a city that pushes the envelope and stretches boundaries. I only wish that people would really take the time to learn an art before they mash it up with other dance forms or theatrical elements. If a spoken word artist contacted me today for a similar show, I would show up in a heartbeat and I would do a much better job this time around. We have to nurture our creative side and experimenting with the non-traditional is ok, but my wish is for people to have enough knowledge to know how to go about it with the right amount of integrity for the art that it blends.

The best way to know if you're ready is when your trusted teacher or mentor starts sharing opportunities with

you. Out of respect for others who are performing, it's a good idea to begin by filling in for dancers and gaining experience before setting up shop and becoming their competition.

II. How to practice like a pro

One of the hardest parts about going pro is that there is less time to focus on practicing. Performance skills and learning to dance through the challenges that sometimes come with gigs are great tools, but nothing takes the place of practice. You'll find that most DVDs are geared toward beginners because they are the largest DVD-buying population. So in addition to classes, workshops and private lessons, how can you ensure that you are refining your technique and continuing to integrate what you've learned? I practice several times a week, and I structure it so that I get the most out of it.

The danger of practice in the YouTube era is the tendency to copy rather than develop your own style. I don't think anyone could express this better than my longtime mentor, Andrea.

I encourage each dancer to find her or his unique voice.

Andrea Beeman, New York City
(www.enchantressofbioluminosity.com)
Photographer: Flaviu Narimba

Andrea, New York City

The Middle Eastern dance genre encompasses many archetypes—temptress, earth mother, sensual goddess, virile gypsy. When dancers express these forms, the link to our dance's historical roots can be felt. Just as a dancer may perform dances inspired by different archetypes, a dancer may also encounter different influences or mentors. In the beginning, the fascination and admiration for this inspirational figure or influential style often translates into a dance of mimicry; the quote "imitation is the sincerest form of flattery" comes to mind. But as this relationship deepens, I encourage each dancer to find her or his unique voice. Discover what it is unique about you and what you bring to the dance. Imitating the performance of Egypt's dance star, Dina, may be a valuable educational tool, but ultimately you want to be YOU when you perform. Finding your unique signature in the dance may take some soul searching and study, or it may come naturally, but it will make you a genuine dance artist.

Early on, practice is focused on attempts to master movements with a seamless flow. Sometimes, however, practice can take a left turn for the aspiring pro. I had a student who discovered Rachel Brice doing a beautiful controlled Turkish drop on YouTube. That became her primary focus and she was intoxicated by the possibility of being able to perform that move. I gave her some strengthening exercises and balance drills to slowly build the technique to perform it safely, but I would catch her in the corner of the studio, going straight to it every chance she got. I would hear a thud, followed by, "I was so close!" Now, this young woman was a dance athlete. She had the flexibility and the strength to study the mechanics and do it perfectly with the right instruction. The Turkish drop was like a "gateway drug" that lured her, but her curiosity expanded and she eventually accepted that challenging movements were only one piece of the puzzle at best. She asked me to recommend books about the history of the dance. I loaned her just about everything in my collection, and she was hungry for more. Initially though, for her and many others, it starts with a desire to perform a movement.

So, in order to get the most out of your practicing and take it beyond the beginner level, here are some tips:

• Divide your time between practice drills and improvisation. Try not to focus solely on one or the other. Play a song that makes you feel great, close your eyes if it helps and just work in some of the movements you enjoy doing. Try to integrate something challenging in one or two spots. For your drills, it's nice to practice in front of a mirror or find a teacher-approved tutorial to follow. Some of the drills I like involve getting out of my head. For example, I will play with concepts like spelling words with my ribcage or playing with level changes from my feet to my head.

• Give yourself a weekly theme. Maybe you want to spend a week developing graceful arms or transitions. This will enable you to go deeper into your vocabulary and allow room for subtlety to develop. Subtlety is an art in and of itself and in my opinion, which is admittedly somewhat jaded, our dance is suffering from a decline in subtlety.

• Practice to a variety of music styles. This will further develop you technique since different music brings out a different movement quality. Practicing snake arms to Arabic pop should feel different than snake arms to an oud taqsim. If you don't know what an oud taqsim is, well, maybe that's a good place to start.

• Grab a practice buddy. I routinely have students who will post on our student Facebook group and ask if anyone wants to get together and work on drum solos or practice a choreography I've taught in class. It's not the same as getting instruction, but it is helpful.

The art of practice will evolve over time and the focus will not remain in mastery of movement alone. When I practice, I inevitably wind up feeling a strong drive to push myself harder. I come away wishing I were better at certain things, and I focus on what I lack compared to the dancers I most admire. It frustrates me, but it also motivates me to keep going. Here's the truth: practice is not necessarily fun. If your goal is to improve, that means you will want to see results and learn to do something differently. Different means pushing yourself and going outside of your comfort zone.

I've come to realize that, at least for me, practice is about developing and learning to strike the right balance of emotion and technique. That balance will not be the same for everyone and that's ok. Maybe I will one day become the dancer who has the arms and hands of Tamalyn Dallal, the focus and artistry of Elena Lentini, the ethereal expression of Mona Said with the fire of Nadia Gamal. In truth, I will probably never reach that level but I intend to have a great time trying.

III. Thoughts on feedback

It is my opinion that dancers should ask for feedback regularly. We should identify the dancers who inspire us, and see if they are open to critiquing or offering feedback. If we rely on post-show compliments as our only cue about our ability, we aren't getting the real picture. Furthermore, feedback from only one person is not the right way to go. Someone who is so familiar with our style might develop dance blind spots, or focus on a particular aspect while unknowingly ignoring others. My approach to seeking and accepting feedback is below. It works for me and, who knows, maybe it will work for you.

Video feedback: I send practice videos to my mentors and pay them to review and provide me with feedback.

Here is some of the feedback I received from my mentor, Andrea, after showing her a practice video.

1. *Finish your opening with a quick spin center before the pro-nounced hip accents. A few moments of heightened energy like that will help the overall dynamics.*

2. *In the section before the 2 minute mark, that might be a good spot to incorporate the diagonals; especially thinking about the upstage portions of them, as you have several downstage V patterns in the piece.*

3. *You're slightly overworking the center forward/downstage backward travel route.*

4. *Try the accents around the 3 minute mark in 4 different directions.*

5. *Add 1 or 2 times where you drop all of the way down to work that lower dynamic a bit more.*

6. *Spice up the last 30 seconds. I think you already mentioned this was a challenge; and the music isn't really telling me anything specific, but try some passes (as in lifting your knee a la ballet) or little kicks. Use the legs and feet a little more in that section in conjunction with the hips.*

Private lessons: I've paid for private lessons with dancers I admire so they could watch me closely and critique as I go. This just cannot happen in a group class situation.

The 24- 48-hour rule: I get what I can only describe as "post-show rawness." Devoting countless hours of practice for a major show and hearing an honest critique immediately after the fact is not a good thing. I am too raw and vulnerable after many performances to appreciate hearing something critical. It's better for me to ask a day or two later when I've got my "tough skin" back on. Someone once said to me, on leaving the venue where I had just performed, "Well, not bad, but not your best." It surprised me because I had a different feeling in my head of what had happened on the stage that night.

Supply prompts: Every so often I have a list of things I'm working on such as dynamics, expressive hands, emotion in movement or some other concept. I might ask a friend, "Can you pay attention to my hands tonight? Specifically, how do they hold up when I'm doing fast hip work?" This gives people an idea of what to focus on and can lead to better results than, "So, how was I?"

IV. Cultivating opportunities

A good way to gain performance experience (and probably score some feedback from professionals in the process) is to attend workshops that allow participants to sign up for a performance slot in a gala show. Frequently, these shows are not easy for lay people to attend because they are long, cramped, and have a fair amount of performances at the non-professional level. Event sponsors need to cover their costs and pay the guest instructor and, believe it or not, semi-pro dancers are often the best draw. Their friends and family haven't yet grown tired of attending their performances, so the novelty hasn't worn off. You can also check your listing for community events, such as town arts fairs or street festivals, to see about performing.

As mentioned earlier, one of my favorite venues to dance at the semi-pro level was at Le Figaro in Greenwich Village. Every week there was a professional dancer-teacher who would have a couple of students do shorter performances to gain experience dancing for an audience and to learn how to dance to live music. The musicians were so nurturing, and they would never get overly fancy or play in a way that was beyond our ability. It was Scott Wilson and a rotating group of musicians that included Raquy, Rami, Carmine, George Stathos, Souren Baronian, Maurice Sedacca and many others. It was the best feeling in the world and the most supportive audience I have ever danced for. Then, the real treat, was watching the final dancer-teacher and see how the experience was elevated.

If there is nothing like Scott Wilson and musicians in your area, consider reaching out to local musicians who might be willing to play for dancers. There are loads of community drum circles, and it could be fun for them and you, to learn Arabic rhythms together. Creating rapport with musicians enhances musicality, reinforces knowledge of rhythms, helps to add dynamics to your dancing and your finger cymbal playing (if you play...and I hope you do).

Another helpful way to get your foot in the door with performances is to reach out to people in the community with whom you have studied with and who you actively support. Let these dancers know that you would be available to fill in for a last-minute slot. It might ease their minds to clarify that you know the etiquette for filling in. So, what is the etiquette when filling in for another dancer's show? I wish I could tattoo this information on my forehead because I hear of people breaking these rules all the time and it's really important to avoid doing that. Dancers will not be invited to return if they don't abide by the following courtesies:

1. When filling in, do not give your card to the owner of the venue. There is no exception to this rule.
2. Do not use specialty props that the venue isn't used to seeing. If the dancer you are covering for doesn't put a hookah pipe on her head, you shouldn't either. It can change the expectation and plant ideas in the owner's mind about what he or she wants at their venue.
3. Do not ask the regular dancer to include you in the rotation (or tell them the owner requested it).

Trust me, you will be taken off a fill-in list faster than you can do a hip drop if you do not follow these guidelines. Earning a solid reputation as an ethical performer who can cover shows without gig poaching will get you so much more work than asserting yourself in inappropriate ways. Keep a gig-bag packed and be ready to say "yes" to those offers even if they mean cancelling other plans at the last minute. Competition is everywhere and the new crop of budding professionals is far greater than the amount of existing work, at least in the Northeast. Of course, there are exceptions and every situation is unique, but keep in mind that you are entering a field and the dancers before you have worked hard to set a standard. Many years ago, I walked into a venue to drop off a card and see if they had bellydancers. I performed, received nice feedback, and then got a furious phone call from a woman who informed me she was the house dancer there. I had no idea because it was never mentioned to me when I went there. Now I am smart enough to know I should explicitly ask if there is a house dancer who does the bookings. It's easier to recover from an honest mistake than it is from shady practices.

Another option for performers who want to immerse themselves in dance is to try and secure a contract working in another country. This is an exciting way to experience various cultures and focus solely on your dancing. Your agent will handle the nuts and bolts of the business, and you can just show up to your performances without having to negotiate payment.

I asked globe-trotting bellydancer, Zaina Brown, what advice she would give to someone considering dancing overseas.

Even the most successful dancers have had their share of difficulties.

Zaina Brown, Globetrotter (https://www.facebook.com/
storiesofatravelingbellydancer)

Zaina, Globetrotter

The dancer who wants to work overseas should be realistic
about her expectations. Competition is fierce. Sometimes,
sadly, looks can matter more than skill. Dancers need to
bring their A-game, street smarts, and have enough money
to survive in case of emergency. Remember that even the
most successful dancers have had their share of difficulties, and push forward!

IV. What's in a name?

As you are building a name for yourself, take care to make sure it's the right one. I have had so many conversations with dancers on this topic and, in the end, my personal opinion is that in some cases it's better to have a dance name that is different from your real name. This isn't always true, but when it matters, it really matters.

Thanks to major search engines and social media, it is harder to build your brand and increase your popularity without a cost to your privacy. When you apply for a job and the company puts your name in a search engine, do you want them to see a YouTube video of you shimmying in a sparkly two piece costume on the first page? Of course, you may feel proud of your dance accomplishments and believe that there is no reason to want to hide that. In truth, I agree with this. But there are certain fields of employment that don't necessarily share my enlightened views.

Don't take my opinion and make it your own. It can also be seen as an advantage to be a dancer who has experience managing clients, meeting expectations, and researching various cultures. A lot of this has to do with your industry and your confidence in speaking about the transferable skills.

A few years ago, I worked for an online marketing company as a freelance content writer. A client called one day after learning that I would be helping to write copy for his new website. His tone on the phone was very accusatory as if he discovered a dirty little secret of mine. The project manager's response was brilliant. She politely explained that not only was I a dancer, but that I was a really talented dancer and the company was very proud of my accomplishments. She reminded the client to focus on my writing samples instead of dance videos that have no relevance to his particular project. Because the company was more interested in working with clients who were not so judgmental about art, this was a personal win for me. I am certain that it could have turned out very differently and could have cost me my job if management had wanted to make the client happy at all costs.

There is also the issue of safety. The world has some unsavory characters and when they latch on to your videos, Facebook pages and websites, they sometimes look for additional avenues into your life. A handful of my dance friends have had stalker situations or creepy fans who lack a healthy set of boundaries. Of course, this is rare, but using your real name is an added level of transparency. I certainly don't want to scare anyone, but it's something to consider. My overly enthusiastic fan was around for only about a month, but it was a tense time and I'm grateful for all the extra security measures that people were willing to take to help me.

Consider your interests, non-dance related goals, your style of dance and costuming to guide your decision about whether or not to choose a dance name. Once you do decide on a name, you'll need to do some research if you want something Arabic. I once had to politely tell a newer dancer who handed me her business card that her name refers to a woman with black hair (she was blonde). Be sure there is not an over-saturation of your chosen name. Some people go around this by adding their location in the title, but this works best when the location is somewhere noteworthy like Cairo. In the great competition for page ranking, if you choose something like Samira, you'll want to consider a last name to go with it. Check the meaning of the name, and run it by a few teachers or friends in the Arabic community to be sure it's appropriate for you.

Another option is to use only your first name, or a slight modification of your first name. For example, Amy can become Amaya. Similarly, a first name with a different last name that is more exotic can work, as well. Be prepared for people asking you where you're from, and "New York" won't work. This is an industry where people are very curious about your background, so consider all of this when choosing your dance name.

1. Stay hydrated and bring snacks. You have to look your best and fading energy can show in the face before it shows in the body.

2. Know your best angles and have a few pre-tested poses so you don't stand there wasting precious time wondering what to do with your arms.

3. If you can't have a stylist on hand, bring a buddy and tell them specifically what to point out. Is a hair out of place? Do you get "back rolls" when your chest isn't lifted enough?

4. Don't overdo it with costume changes. That is precious time you could be spending with your photographer getting the right shot. I generally bring two to three looks per shoot.

5. Choose your photographers wisely and then trust them. Like most things, you get what you pay for so beware of bargains. Get to know your photographer's aesthetic and try to ensure it's a good fit. If a photographer has a noir/gloomy style and you want super smiley images with a happy white backdrop, keep searching.

Opposite:
Tava & Sira by Joe Marquez, The Smoking Camera

I. Budget time and money for the costs ahead

It used to be that in order become professional, you worked your way into a venue and performed. An audience member who enjoyed your show would get your contact information and book you for another show. Word of mouth might increase your popularity to the point where you have an agent or book shows internationally. Based on talent and charismatic performances, the scene decided which dancers became popular. Costumes were often made by dancers and they were rich, intricate and personalized.

Today, most dancers have to spend money on a professional website (which includes hosting fees, domain name registry, design fees and SEO packages if the dancer chooses); marketing materials, such as business cards and flyers; professional photo shoots, video editors, music editors, professional costuming; and the list goes on and on. The time investment for social media, networking and editing photos or videos means that being a dancer is equal to running a small business without the budget to afford much help.

Maria, an award-winning dancer from California, has some terrific advice about the business aspects of bellydance:

I did my research and ended up choosing the dancer who had the best website.

Maria, California (www.orientdancer.com)
Photographer: Michael Baxter

Being a professional bellydancer requires the skill of com-
bining art and business. When you make your living and
support yourself entirely with dancing, you have no choice
but to put effort into building your "small business." I
am lucky to be able to use my artistic side and business
degree. I am forever grateful to my teacher, who not only
taught me dance technique, but who also generously guid-
ed me through establishing myself with her wise advice
and useful tips. Here are some tips I picked to share that
may help to build your brand as a dancer.

*Website: Make a strong first impression and have easily
accessible information.*

When I became interested in bellydancing and was looking for a teacher in the area, I did my research and ended
up choosing the dancer who had the best website. Why
was it best? It had professional pictures, artistic graph-
ics, and clear information. I said to myself, "Wow!" I
believe people looking for a dancer to hire go through a
similar process when they do research. There should be
a short bio, awards and achievements, photos, videos,
teaching schedule, performance listing, and booking information. Keep it short and easy. After all, it is your
business card on the Internet. Make sure to have a menu
structure that is simple. Most information should be

accessible within two clicks because people often lose patience when forced to dig deep for relevant content. Some dancers include additional informative content like blogs, forums and articles. I forced myself to learn basic HTML web design through books and online resources. After many sleepless nights of testing and editing, the feeling of excitement from the results makes it all worthwhile.

Social networks: Maintain a business image, but don't forget to add a personal touch.

Sometimes I wish I could hire a person to maintain my three Facebook pages, Twitter, Google+, YouTube, and others. It's a lot of work—and it's work that might seem like a waste of time to some. In my case, I get local gig bookings and referrals through Facebook as well as inquires about traveling to perform and teach workshops internationally. It is a powerful networking tool. The key is to have content to share, and to do it consistently. Adding a bit of personal content allows people who follow you to learn what kind of person you are. Someone might like you for your pretty pictures, someone for your funny jokes, but no one will if you are just a promotion machine. You also need to update your page regularly because these sites calculate your popularity indexes, and if you abandon it for a long time, your index will go down resulting in lower post visibility.

Printed promotional materials: Business cards, flyers for classes, event posters and more.

Perhaps you don't use all of these, but having professional-looking business cards is a must. They should be on heavy-weight paper with glossy finish, double-sided with professional photos, and legible contact information. I do my own design in Photoshop and then send it to a printing company. I always carry some in my purse to give to clients. I also keep a stack at the front desk of the restaurants where I perform. Often people pick them up just as a souvenir on their way out, or if the card is nice looking they don't throw it away. Sooner or later it may lead you to a gig or referral.

Photos: Professional studio photos and performance shots.

Since I was a student, I have always invested in professional photos. Being a model in the studio turned out to be a tough and exhausting job, and posing is a complicated skill! My recommendation is to learn Photoshop because, ultimately, no one knows your taste better than you do. You should, at least, be able to perform simple manipulations like cropping and changing brightness and contrast. More advanced photo retouching and background graphic design is also a very useful skill. I bought a book, opened the program and gradually learned it by experimenting and practicing. Having performance shots in your portfolio is very important, too, because you don't want to look like a virtual dancer with just glamorous shots. You need to show that you are a working artist and allow people to see how you look in real settings.

Videos: Variety and consistency.

It's nice to have a variety of videos in your portfolio—from theater performances and restaurants, both choreographed and improvised; footage from competitions and some that show you dancing with the crowd. It's also nice having all sides of your talent shown, so include drum solo performances, lyrical songs, veils, and folklore. Maintain your Youtube channel as if it's your dance resume (and in fact it is). You want to show all your experience and skills and have a well-rounded balanced image of yourself presented. The consistency of strategy will keep your audience engaged. If you have five new videos, don't post them all in one day and then have a zero YouTube activity for the next six months. Keep it spaced out, like a magazine subscription. Make sure you have your name and website in the video titles, as eventually they will get reposted and lose the original information, so it's good to have your name embedded in the video itself. Share your video in social networks for more visibility.

I couldn't agree more with Maria's business breakdown. People are often under the impression that dancers spend all their time dancing. The truth is, we have a choice between spending our time learning these skills ourselves or paying someone to do it for us. I wind up doing about 90% myself, but I rely on professionals for the things I haven't mastered yet or simply cannot do. For example, I love when friends come to my shows and I don't often want to burden them with the task of filming. It's also not as easy as it may seem. For high-stakes shows, I would rather pay a videographer who can guarantee that I am in the center of the frame, keep the camera steady, and refrain from adding verbal commentary while they film me. In many cases, this expense may be almost as much as I am paid to perform in a show, but having the show on video will also serve as fresh content for the social media outlets.

I would also like to add a bit about keeping track of finances. Lately, I am performing at more corporate events and galas with businesses that prefer to pay by check or credit card. This means holding onto receipts and having an accountant you can trust. If numbers are your thing and you can do it yourself with a tax program, hats off to you. It is not my strength and there is too much room for error. Consider hiring an accountant once your career goes beyond counting out cash and tips.

II. Costuming

One of the obvious ways we elevate our performance value as a professional is with high quality costuming. A random skirt with a hip scarf and fancy top can take you far, but at this level you will want to invest in something beaded or delve into costuming that is appropriate for certain music. Do you want a galabeya, Khaleji thobe or a complete bedlah for your performance? Who will you be dancing for and how conservative are they? These are questions to consider when buying and choosing costumes.

Most people wind up buying a matching bra and belt set for their first costume. It is best to choose a popular and versatile color, like red or gold, with elements that can be mixed and matched to create new looks. My first costume was a Turkish beaded bra and belt that I wore with a variety of skirts and accessories that were easy to pair with other dancer's costumes for group shows or duets. Furthermore, something as simple as switching a velvet mermaid skirt for a full chiffon skirt in a different complementary color really increased the mileage I got out of a few basic pieces.

It must be stated that purchases at this level, while much shinier and more striking than the skirt with hip scarf look, may not be very well made. I learned the hard way not to trust seams and hooks. My very first paid bellydance performance was a horror story of mangled safety pins and near wardrobe malfunction. Please do yourself a favor and reinforce wherever the straps are sewn onto the bra and use a thick upholstery thread for tightening all hooks. A good seamstress can help if you lack adequate sewing skills like I do. My seamstress has become an integral part of my team and I dread the day when she moves and I needed to build a rapport like that from scratch. She has been one of the greatest finds of my career.

Another option is to scour the bellydance swapmeet pages online and find something pre-owned. It's a nice way to get a more professional costume for less money than a new one may cost. If a costume is well cared for, it has a lot of dancing life left in it after the first or even the second owner. I have been the second owner for many a costume and it has given me the ability to rotate my costume collection so it's always fresh. If a venue starts to recognize your costumes, you run the risk of seeming too familiar. A costume rotation sends the message that you are in demand and can offer variety.

At a certain point, the style of costumes changed and I wanted to get away from the heavy fringe and bra/belt sets I had grown accustomed to. Some of the designers I enjoy are Eman Zaki, Pharonics of Egypt, Hoda Zaki, Shahraman Palace and Bella. I particularly appreciate that Bella makes art out of my rough ideas and sketches. I can write her and say something like, "I want something snakeskin that is elegant enough for a princess. Here are some design inspirations." Boom. In three months, there's a box at my door. The bottom line is, wear what makes you feel great and make sure it suits your shape and height. Just because a design is expensive doesn't mean it's right for you. What looks playful and exciting on one dancer can look like a tacky birthday cake when it's on my short frame. It's a good idea to seek out well-known dancers with your body type and see what looks good on them.

As you're choosing costumes, please consider your style of dancing to be sure it's an appropriate pairing. A lycra skirt with a high slit is not the best choice if you plan to do floorwork. Your costume choice tells your audience what to expect from your performance so if you enter a room with a Turkish-inspired beaded fringe bedlah, and perform Modern Egyptian style, it might confuse people.

If you will dance on a raised stage, be mindful that a full skirt will lift as you spin. (Oh, the things I've seen). If you can't resist doing splits, please to be sure you aren't flashing crotch. Even if your costume has shorts sewn in, it isn't immediately clear to your audience that they aren't getting a full view of your underwear. And, lastly, I was trained never to have crotch towards the audience for backbends or floorwork. I'm sure there are artistic exceptions but, consider the messages that your movements, in conjunction with your costuming, send to your audience before you accept money for performances. Don't worry too much about this because if you carry yourself as an elegant professional dancer, mishaps are more easily forgiven.

There are many directories and sources for online for costume sales. Here are a few places to start your search:

- Bhuz
- eBay
- Facebook groups dedicated to costume sales
- Sign up for mailing lists of individual dancers that regularly rotate their costume collection.

A lot of secondhand purchases may require adjustments that are beyond your level of expertise. In your quest for a qualified seamstress, contact a local theater group to see who they use, or reach out to a ballroom dance school. It is a delicate art and, believe me, the last thing you want is a wardrobe malfunction.

I have the highest respect for people who can make their own costumes. It's not necessarily cheaper, considering the cost of materials and the time to make them, however, a unique design that fits perfectly is a beautiful thing. Hats off to you talented sewing folks for raising the bar. I have watched friends making their own costumes and witnessed their neck pain and bleeding fingers. It is all really impressive.

Rotation vs. hoarding

I get it. Costumes contain certain memories that we get attached to. It's hard to let them go. Some people have the luxury of large closets, so they can keep accumulating rather than rotating. Most dancers I know will rotate their collection instead of continually adding to it. If you purchase a costume that you intend to sell, you must care for it. Be mindful of wearing these costumes in places with smoke, pet hair, or dirty floors that can stain the bottom of a skirt. I have some costumes that I wear only for galas or weddings (and other clean and smoke-free places). I used to tack the skirt so it would still be long enough to sell to a wide selection of people, but now that I've found enough people my height, I can shorten my skirts for a better fit. These are all things to consider when buying a costume you may, ultimately, sell.

Even if you have a growing collection, you still must care for them. Sitting in a closet unattended may be just as harmful as wearing costumes in hookah bars. Store your costumes in breathable fabric bags whenever possible. Be sure to have a dry storage area to help prevent mildew growth. It's best not to hang them because the fabric will stretch over time if there is elastic or lycra. Lastly, if you have pets, make sure they don't have access to the place where you keep your costumes. I have a pair of Isis wings full of tiny tooth holes from my old cat Satchmo (RIP). There are countless stories of cats peeing in gig bags and one dog I know who shredded a veil.

Photography: Bill Winters

I have two costumes that I never wear and they sit in my closet for the sake of nostalgia. One is the first costume I ever bought and the other is a long fringed number that belonged to several other dancers before me. One day, they will have to go but I'm just not ready yet.

Caring for costumes

After you perform, fold or gently roll your costume to return it to your bag. When you get home, be sure to remove the costume so it can dry out from sweat or restaurant odors. If you don't do this, you will have a wrinkled costume that is slightly damp (and crawling with bacteria) and it will smell like Moroccan food, smoke, sweat, or whatever else you encountered during your show.

There are several methods for cleaning costumes, but for general care, I usually dab my bra and belt lining with diluted vodka, lemon and lavender essential oil. That coupled with a little time in the sun and it's good as new. If a lining is really showing signs of dirt or wear, I will ask my seamstress to insert a new lining. Washing can be tricky because the colors may bleed, but you can do a test with cold water and a very gentle soap. I also hang my costumes gently while I shower to "steam" them.

The biggest problem area is the bottom of the skirt, which can pick up dirt from a venue's floor. I do a periodic soak, but you do run the risk of a slightly lighter color from this cleaning, depending on your fabric. The steamer helps to deodorize it but won't necessarily remove a dirt stain.

You'll just have to decide which is worse and take care not to drag a light colored skirt on the floor too much, particularly if you want to sell it.

When a costume isn't drying or airing out, I store mine in a canvas fabric bag with a clear plastic front. This enables me to see my collection while allowing the costume to breathe. Chiffon is easier to hang and bras can be kept on hangers but I have more shelf space than hanging space and that's part of why I prefer the bags. My veils are gently rolled (not folded) and kept in a canvas shoe storage hanger. I also keep some rolled in a larger fabric bag.

Miki, Kansas, (student) had this to say about her first costume purchase:

Miki, Kansas

Buying a professional costume for the first time was an exciting and terrifying experience. I ordered the costume online, and although I had painstakingly measured exactly as described, when the costume finally arrived, the skirt was too small and the bra all but hung off me. Fortunately, I had the contact of a great seamstress who helped me make the adjustments AND I allotted time for her to do the alterations. The costume ended up fitting perfectly and I have worn it now multiple times using different layers. Getting the right fit was absolutely key. I'll never order a costume again expecting that it will fit right out of the box!"

III. The good and bad of directories

There are a number of online directories that you can pay to be listed in. Some are better than others, but the experiences of my fellow dancers vary too much to say that one is unanimously bad or good. The advantage of joining a directory is exposure to clients on a platform that is user-friendly. The disadvantage of joining a directory is that a client might wind up choosing a dancer based on his or her fee and that can promote undercutting and direct competition.

My preference is to talk with someone, ask all the questions I need answered so that I know what to charge, and also feel comfortable negotiating before I enter into an agreement. Using a directory, I may bid on a gig and then "poof" the client has paid me a deposit before we've even had a conversation. I have noticed that a lot of these platforms now give the option to request additional information before bidding, and this is a step in the right direction. I also notice that a lot of dancers are eager to bid without all the information, and a client won't necessarily take the time to answer your questions when they are presented with five to ten women who are ready to dance regardless.

On occasion, you will receive such random requests as "We are looking for a bellydancer who is at least 5'7", with black hair, to jump out of a cake at a birthday party." (Yes, that is an actual request that I received). You'll have to determine how much time and effort you spend bidding on these inquiries. In short, directories can lead to additional bookings, but they are far from perfect. Read reviews before joining and talk to dancers to get a sense of their experiences with various directories.

I. Suggestions for staying inspired

So far, we've painted a picture of a professional dancer's life that includes the need for a variety of skill sets, such as photo editing, video editing, sewing, HTML, and a significant financial investment for marketing, costuming and continued training. We've talked about the time away from family and friends, the physical strain on the body and the reality that it doesn't last. Now that the nuts and bolts are out of the way, let's get to the good part! If it were all sacrifices and demands, nobody would do it. If you're reading this book, it's because you love to dance and getting paid to do it is a dream come true.

Sometimes it's easy to forget how much we love it because we can turn into gig-chasers or find ourselves doing performances that feed our wallets more than our hearts. Once you rely on income from dance jobs, it's not as easy to carve out time for the parts we love. But it is really important to do it so that you avoid burnout, injury, and remain artistically satisfied.

Whether your career involves weekly gigs in your area, teaching jobs at various studios, or you are fortunate enough to carve a name for yourself in the workshop circuit, we cannot really do our job well if we're not inspired to dance.

Here are some suggestions:

1. Take breaks. It's not easy, but every so often take a weekend off, a vacation, or stay home and nurture your non-dance identity.

2. Be in the audience. I try my best to go and watch my favorite dancers perform for the dose of inspiration and reminders of why I fell in love with this dance. I also get so much love from my community and friends. And a bonus benefit is that these dancers may be more likely to return the favor and attend your shows.

3. Audition for a professional dance company. I have had the honor and privilege of being a part of Caravanserai Dance Theater. Elena Lentini is inspiration personified. Her vision and approach to movement always take me out of my comfort zone and transport me somewhere very different and exciting.

4. Try a new costume that brings out a different quality of movement.

5. Make sure you aren't performing to the same playlist so often that it no longer inspires you. Change your music as often as you can.

6. Seek a mentor. Being around dancers who have more experience than you is both humbling and inspiring. Good hearty chats about what keeps them going can feed your passion for days.

7. Dive into the cultural connection. Get out of the flashy parts and explore the rich lineage. I think this is essential because it will cultivate a respect for the art and help you see the value in what you do.

8. Seek opportunities to dance to live music. The chemistry between dancer and musician really fans the flames. Live music gets you out of your head and into the experience. It is intoxicating!

But the real answer to staying inspired is staying true to yourself.

Angelica Jordan, Québec, (www.AngelicaDance.com) had this to say about staying inspired:

Angelica, Québec

Getting tangled in a web of drama in this industry seems almost inevitable, and so is turning inward on a regular basis to remember why it is that I (or you) started to dance is crucial. And so I am most inspired when my heart is in the right place. I have always been fascinated by world religion and culture and find an unstoppable passion pouring out of me when I delve into researching more about the Arab world and its art. Whether it be the dance, the music, the poetry, the language, the religion, or even the food; I am in heaven! The moment I lose sight of my curiosity is usually linked with the moment I get caught up with all of the hardships that come with making a living as a full time professional dancer. Taking a break is necessary sometimes, but the real answer to staying inspired is staying true to yourself, whoever you may be.

Communication and compromise are often necessary to collaborate successfully.

Photography: Raya Photography

Working with other dancers is very rewarding on many levels. Gigs with other dancers are often the most fun to do, provided your dance partners are easygoing, professional and don't feel the need to outshine others. Whether you are performing choreography on a stage or improvising together, it's important to remember that you're working as a team. Every dancer has a different movement style and presence, so you still bring your own unique qualities, but it's more pleasing to the eye when parts (in this case dancers) work together as a whole. Let's put it this way, don't throw in a Turkish drop at the end of a set unless you know your partner(s) will do the same.

In addition to sharing attention, dancing with a partner (or partners) also fosters a team approach to splitting tips evenly. This way, nobody feels envious if another dancer happens to get the happy-tipping table. When choosing to work with other dancers you are entering a relationship. That means communication and compromise are necessary for successful collaboration. This is evident when coming together to choreograph a number. One person can steer the ship, but all parties involved should be able to contribute his/her opinions or ideas. I've been blessed in knowing a group of dancers with whom I have worked for years and trust. If you work together enough, it becomes easier to improvise because you become more familiar with their vocabulary of movements. And if you're really lucky, you'll find a doppelganger as I have found in working with Tava!

II. The awkward pairing of art and commerce

I'm sure this could be an entire book, but I'll have to settle for a small section here. People who dance for the love of the art have a challenging transition ahead of them when it comes to dancing for work. Instead of allowing ourselves to move freely with the sole purpose of artistic integrity, we are hired to do a job. The focus is on doing our jobs well, so that we have happy clients and can earn our living or supplement our income. Like many, I started teaching just to be able to afford classes and workshops and I stayed there for years. Over time, I started to perform regularly because I thought, "Hey, why not get paid to practice?" I loved developing those gig skills like getting people to clap and learning how to pace myself for three or four 30-minute sets. I fell in love with the adrenaline and the excitement, but I also learned that some people can be really cruel. There is no denying how awful it feels when an audience ignores you, disrespects you, or douses you in champagne (true story).

There are times when a client will call and say, "Hi Tava. You danced at my friend's wedding and I really loved your show. It was elegant and entertaining. Would you dance at my wedding?" And there are many other times when I'll get a call that goes more like this, "Hi. I need a dancer for my party. These are my colors, so you have to match. I also want lots of fire and Isis wings. Make sure you look your best and wear high heels if you're not tall." Sometimes the best paydays are the ones that have the least artistry. All I can say is this, keep in mind that you are in the business of customer service when you are performing. Your client negotiations are very important because the more you represent yourself as a business person, the more likely you are to earn the respect of your clients, (and help them understand why your rate is justified).

It can start to feel like we are some kind of sparkly product. A lot of clients will want the splashy feel of entertainment without the soul we long to express. You will be confronted with people's insecurities, stereotypes and judgments. When you pair art with money, it is understood that you meet an expectation and this requires a completely different mindset when you perform. Going into your performance life with eyes wide open and allowing plenty of opportunity to dance purely for the love of it will save you lots of frustration down the road. You will learn to find the joy in most dance experiences. When your job is to bring joy to a group, it is often rewarding even if you are dancing with props you don't love, or if you're missing out on time with your significant other.

Be open to surprises because sometimes a job that you expect to be "for the paycheck" may turn into a delightful evening. And the opposite is sometimes true, as well. I pull up to a venue and I set an intention before I get out of the car. If my mood is sour or if I've given up some fun thing to do in order to do my job, it's important that I remind myself how fortunate I am to be working, creating a joyful experience for others, and that it is an honor to be in this role. Recently I saw something very disturbing on my way to a show. I sat in my car, trying not to let the tears ruin my makeup. I gave myself a pep talk and had one of the greatest performance experiences of my entire career. The audience was so fantastic that I left feeling completely exhilarated. We are so lucky to do what we do!

'd like to thank each of you for caring enough to read these words. Every new reader means that someone else wants to represent bellydance in the best possible light and that is a good thing.

I'll be honest, part of my motivation for writing this came from watching or hearing about dancers who undercut, wear inappropriate costuming, or engage in other offensive behaviors. I'm a firm believer in flipping a frustration so that it can lead to something positive. I could call my friends and gripe, or I could do something about it! So, I hope you found this worthy of your time. This is certainly not meant to be an exhaustive how-to guide, and it could never take the place of a mentor, but I hope it's a step in the right direction toward helping dancers make informed choices.

I certainly haven't figured it all out, and it took me a few years to work up the courage to write these words. I had to quiet my inner voice that said, "Who are you to be putting this information out? So many dancers have been doing this longer than you. So many dancers know more than you do!" In the end, I decided I cared enough to take the risk and I know that this is only one voice among many. You should read them all. Every perspective will lead to greater professionalism.

Being a professional bellydancer can be a bumpy ride, but it has brought me tremendous satisfaction even though it regularly tests my dedication, endurance and skill. I want each of us to thrive and squash those awful and misleading stereotypes so that we won't be thought of as lascivious jiggle-bots. We owe it to our art to read every book we can find, take every class and workshop we can afford, research on our own, and work to elevate the perceptions of bellydancers.

Lastly, I want to offer my sincerest thanks to Jewel Moulthrop for all of her edits. Without her, this guidebook would be particularly short on commas, and chock full of exaggerations that favor flair over making sense. Additional thanks go to Andrea, Angelica, Maria, Miki, Riskallah, and Zaina, for their contributions. My teachers, dance friends and colleagues inspire me every day and continue to raise the bar. I am in awe of my community. Now go dance your heart out and remind yourself why you do this. Leave your audience with raw hands from clapping so vigorously. Move someone to tears with your artistry. And never sell yourself short.

RESOURCES AND LINKS

Costume Resources:
https://www.bellydancestore.biz/
http://www.Bhuz.com
http://www.Dahlal.com
Facebook Bellydance Costume Swap

Costume Designers:
http://www.bellacostumes.com/
https://www.etsy.com/shop/EshtaAmar
http://shahramanpalace.com/
Atelier Christtiano Ferreira
http://www.eman-zaki.com/

Arabic Dance Education & Teacher Training:
Bellyqueen's Teacher Training: http://bellyqueen.com/
events/workshops/teachers-training/
Sahra C. Kent's extensive course: http://
journeythroughegypt.com/
Tamalyn Dallal offers teacher training workshops:
http://www.tamalyndallal.com/
Yasmina Ramzy's Arabesque Academy:
http://www.arabesquedance.ca/yasmina/teaching.php

Dancers who contributed quotes:
Andrea – http://www.enchantressofbioluminosity.com
Angelica – http://www.angelicadance.com
Maria – www.orientdancer.com
Riskallah – http://www.riskallah.com
Sira - www.BellydancerNYC.com
Zaina - https://www.facebook.com/
storiesofatravelingbellydancer

Keep in Touch with Tava:
Facebook.com/TavaBellydancer
Twitter: @dancingtava
Blog: dancingtava.wordpress.com
YouTube: https://www.youtube.com/user/dancingtava
Pinterest: https://www.pinterest.com/dancingtava/
Instagram: dancingtava
http://www.BellydancebyTava.com
To learn more about Tava's mentorship program, visit
http://bellydancebytava.com/mentorship-program/

Good Reads:
You Asked Aunt Rocky: Answers & Advice about Raqs
Sharqi and Raqs Shaabi
by Morocco (C Varga Dinicu)

The Bellydance Handbook: A Companion for the
Serious Dancer
by Princess Farhana

A Trade Like Any Other
by Karin Van Nieuwkerk

Grandmother's Secrets: The Ancient Rituals and
Healing Power of Belly Dancing
by Rosina Fawzia al-Rawi

23737202R00049

Made in the USA
San Bernardino, CA
29 August 2015